BEHIND THE SCENES

MUSIC

Frances Ridley

Editorial Consultant – Cliff Moon

RISING ★ STARS

nasen
NASEN House, 4/5 Amber Business Village, Amber Close,
Amington, Tamworth, Staffordshire B77 4RP

Rising Stars UK Ltd.
22 Grafton Street, London W1S 4EX
www.risingstars-uk.com

Every effort has been made to trace copyright holders and
obtain their permission for use of copyright material. The
publisher will gladly receive information enabling them to
rectify any error or omission in subsequent editions.
All facts are correct at time of going to press.

First published 2006

Cover design: Button plc
Cover image: Alamy
Illustrator: Bill Greenhead
Text design and typesetting: Marmalade Book Design
(www.marmaladebookdesign.com)
Educational consultants: Cliff Moon and Lorraine Petersen
Technical consultant: Patrick Walton
Pictures: Alamy: pages 8-9, 18, 22, 23, 25, 26, 38, 39, 41, 46
Empics: pages 4, 10, 11, 14, 15, 23, 36, 37, 42-43
Rex: pages 4, 5, 17, 26, 27, 29, 37, 39

British Library Cataloguing in Publication Data.
A CIP record for this book is available from the British
Library.

ISBN: 978-1-84680-049-8

Contents

Starting out

There are no rules in the music business.

Every act has a different story.

Will Young won 'Pop Idol' in 2002.
He has become a famous pop singer.

Before

After

Before

Charlotte Church sang **classical** songs. Now she's crossed over to pop!

After

The Coral started out at school.

Alan Wills used to be the drummer in Shack. He heard The Coral play.

He liked them so much he set up a record label for them!

Reth are an **extreme metal** band from Burnley.

Patrick – singer

Jim – guitar

Paul – bass

Elliot – drums

Band fact!

The word 'reth' comes from Africa. It means 'king'.

The story so far ...

2000 – two school friends start Reth.

Reth play gigs and **support** bigger bands.

Reth get better at writing and playing songs.

2006 – Reth record an album and play an 8-day UK tour.

The story continues ...

The band hope a record label will sign them.

They say: "The time has now come for Reth!"

Getting signed

Most bands hope a record label will sign them.

Record labels help them to market and sell records.

Record labels send A&R people to look for new bands.

A&R people look for songs that will sell and bands that work hard.

A&R fact!

'A&R' stands for 'Artists and Repertoire' — that means the acts and the records they make!

A&R people listen to **demos** and go to gigs.

They check out lots of bands.

They advise the record label which bands to sign.

A&R people then look after the signed bands.

Arctic Monkeys

In 2004, Arctic Monkeys put **demos** of their music on the Internet.

Fans downloaded them for free.

Word spread fast. The music press wrote about the band.

Arctic Monkeys gigs sold out. A&R people were not on the guest list!

Arctic Monkeys made their first EP in 2005. Most fans downloaded it from iTunes.

Two months later, Arctic Monkeys signed with the Domino record label.

Arctic Monkeys got signed without A&R!

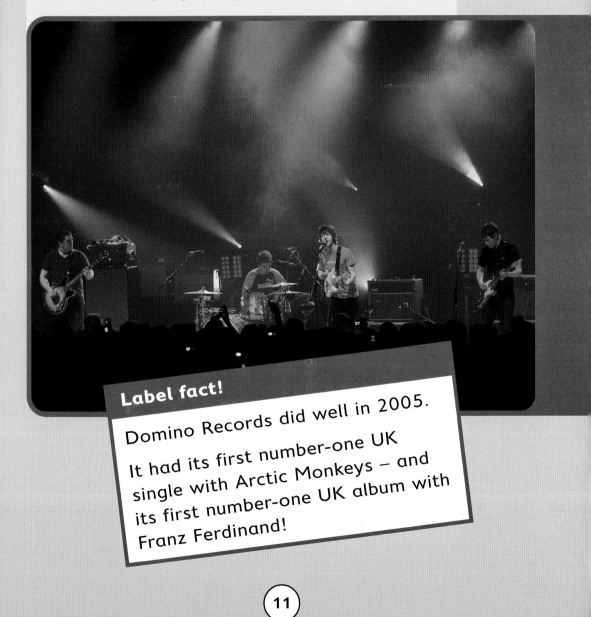

Label fact!

Domino Records did well in 2005.

It had its first number-one UK single with Arctic Monkeys — and its first number-one UK album with Franz Ferdinand!

Kickbox (Part one)

The band was Seb's idea.

"It's so easy!" said Seb. "Mark on guitar, Rick on drums, me singing. Kickbox is formed!"

"Kickbox?" asked Mark.

"Why not?" said Seb.

There was no stopping Seb. He booked a **rehearsal** room.

"Ten o'clock Saturday," he said. "Don't be late!"

Seb was already setting up when I got there.

"You're late," he said. It was only five past ten!

Then Mark walked in – with a girl!

"Who's *that*?" said Seb.

Mark looked hurt. The girl looked bored.

"This is Megan," said Mark. "She won't be any trouble. Hey, I've got some songs!"

"Cool," I said. "When did you start writing songs?"

Mark went red and started to say something. But Seb butted in.

"Come on!" he said. "It's ten past ten already!"

Continued on page 20

Writing songs

Many bands write their own songs – but not all acts do.

A songwriter does it for them.

Max Martin is a famous songwriter and producer. He has written songs for Britney Spears, Backstreet Boys and Pink.

Missy Elliott is a songwriter, a producer and a rapper.

Guy Chambers wrote many hit songs with Robbie Williams.

Reth on songwriting

Elliot and Jim write the songs for Reth. The band play each song in **rehearsal**.

They practise until everyone is happy.

Playing live

Most bands play live gigs. Bands with a good **fan base** go on tours.

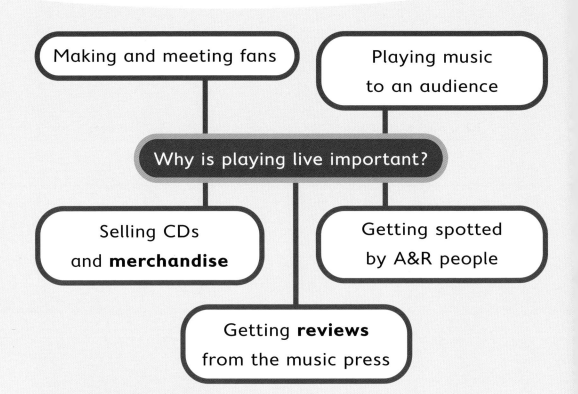

Making and meeting fans

Playing music to an audience

Why is playing live important?

Selling CDs and **merchandise**

Getting spotted by A&R people

Getting **reviews** from the music press

Reth on tour

Reth toured with three other bands in a huge van. They stayed with fans and promoters. They say: "Gigs are a great advertisement for us. We sell home-made **demo** CDs. If fans like the **demo**, they may buy the album!"

Big bands like Kaiser Chiefs go on worldwide tours to reach their fans and sell records.

Kaiser Chiefs Tours 2006

April–October UK and European tour

Results

Three BRIT Awards, 2006

Two NME Awards, 2006

Worldwide album sales – 3.67 million

Booking agent

A booking agent books the **venues** for bands. It's important to choose **venues** that are good for the band.

Roadies

Roadies move and look after the equipment on tour. They look after the instruments, lighting, sound and stage.

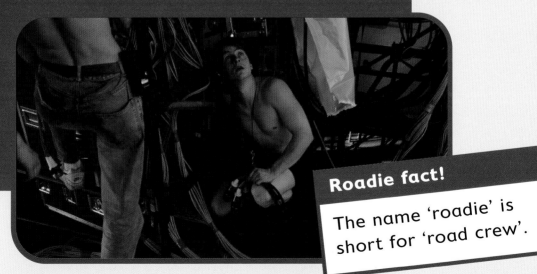

Roadie fact!

The name 'roadie' is short for 'road crew'.

Reth tour notes

Two good things about tours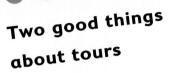

- Playing to new people in different towns.
- Making new friends and having fun with other bands.

Two bad things about tours

- Travelling for hours.
- Sleeping on floors and settees.

Kickbox (Part two)

The **rehearsal** went well. The songs were great. Mark was good on guitar. I wasn't bad on drums. But there was a problem …

Seb was rubbish.

His voice was too soft and he was a really bad dancer.

"What did you think?" said Seb after the **rehearsal**.

"It was OK," I said. "But …"

"But what?" he said.

"Nothing," I said. "It was great."

Kickbox did more **rehearsals**. Mark wrote more songs. My drumming got better. Seb's singing didn't.

But there was no stopping Seb.

"We've got loads of songs," he said. "Let's do a gig."

Seb worked like a demon. He booked a **venue**. He got posters and badges. He advertised in the paper and on the Internet. Everyone was talking about Kickbox.

Continued on page 30

Recording songs

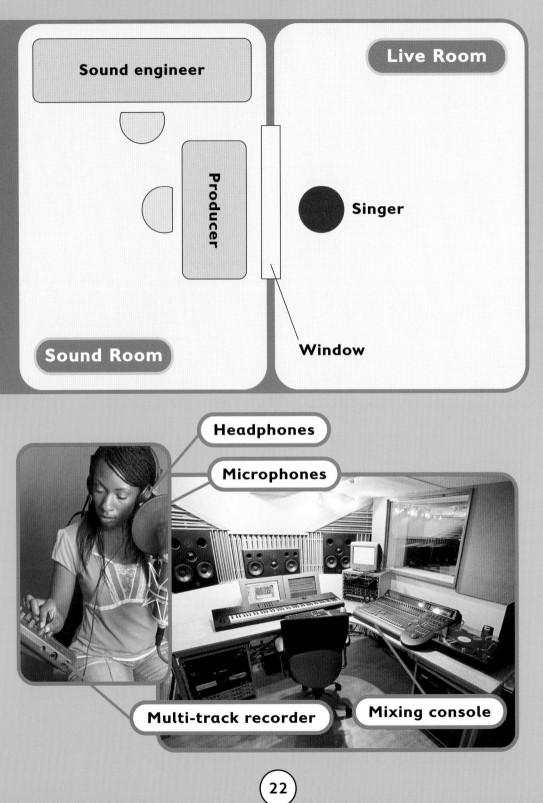

Sound engineer

Live Room

Producer

Singer

Sound Room

Window

Headphones

Microphones

Multi-track recorder

Mixing console

22

Producers and sound engineers

Producers:

- get the best out of the songs

- get the best out of the performers

- get the best out of the recording session.

Sound engineers:

- set up the equipment

- record each track

- mix the tracks on tape

- make a **master** of the recordings.

Recording fact!

Each part of the music is recorded separately. The headphones play the rest of the music to the performer. This helps them to keep in time – and in tune!

Recording at home

Mike 'Spike' Stent is a sound engineer.
He has worked for Madonna, Oasis and U2.
He says: "Some of the best records ever made
were done in people's bedrooms."

Jyoti 'White Town' Mishara
recorded 'Your Woman' in his
bedroom. He sent out five
copies. The record was played
on Radio 1 and it went to
number one in the UK chart!

Mike 'The Streets' Skinner
recorded his first album in
his bedroom. He was living
with his mum at the time!

The White Stripes recorded their first album in the lead singer's living room.

Cocorosie recorded their first album in a bathtub!

Band facts!

Most **demo** recordings are home-made.

The Bees recorded their first album in a shed.

Getting noticed

There are a lot of new acts, but only a few acts will make it.

They need people to find out about their music.

They need people to hear their music.

That's where the media come in!

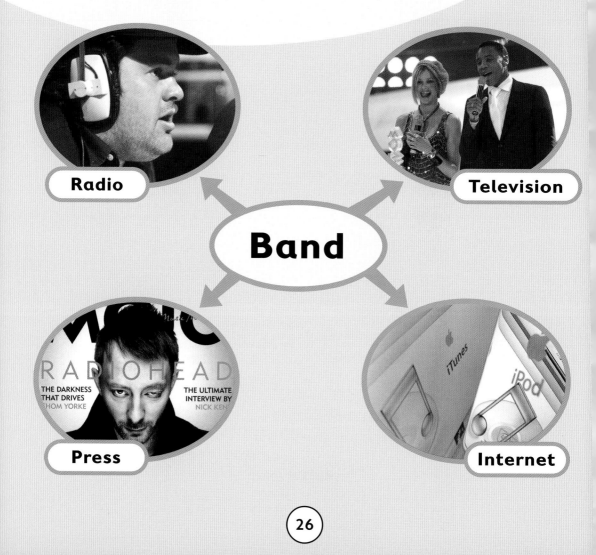

Radio

Television

Band

Press

Internet

Record promoter

It's not easy to get the media on your side. Many bands ask a record promoter to help. A record promoter gets new records played on radio and in clubs. He gets the band on television and in the music press. He promotes the band online.

Talk the talk!

Airtime – The amount of times that a record is played on radio and television.

Plugging – Getting airtime for new records is called 'plugging'.

Music journalists and radio DJs

The music press and radio are important to new bands.

Music promoters send free recordings to music journalists and DJs.

Music journalists write about music in magazines and on websites.

They **review** records and gigs.

They **interview** bands and singers.

DJs play music and talk about it on air.

DJ Steve Lamacq is famous for helping new bands.

In 2003, he made Keane's first record his 'Single of the Week'.

Keane sold all 500 copies and did a sell-out tour.

Soon after, they were signed by Island Records.

Keane

Kickbox (Part three)

There were loads of kids outside the gig.

Seb went white. He said: "I can't do this!"

"Don't be stupid!" I said. "You have to!"

"Yeah," said Mark. "There're loads of kids outside. You have to sing."

"No," said Seb. "I can't sing. I can't dance. I can't do this gig."

Seb had made up his mind. What were we going to do?

"I'll sing," said Megan.

"*What*?" shouted Seb. "*You*? You don't care about Kickbox. You just sit around looking bored. I bet you can't even remember the songs!"

"I do care," said Megan. "I act bored so I don't put you off. I saw that you were shy about singing. As for the songs – I wrote them!"

Mark went red. But Seb didn't care. He shouted: "Great! You're on!"

Continued on the next page

The gig was brilliant. Megan had a great voice – loud and gritty. She could dance, too. And she was good at getting the crowd going!

I played those drums like a maniac. And Mark is a great guitarist – even if he didn't write the songs!

And Seb? He didn't waste his time.

He talked to a journalist from the local newspaper ...

... a DJ from the local radio ...

... and a record producer from a local studio ...

Kickbox had only just got started!

Marketing music

New records come out every week.

Good marketing aims the record at the people who will buy it!

Marketing people **package** the record. They:

- sort out the artwork on the record sleeve

- plot the best time for the record to come out

- stir up media interest in the record.

Marketing people also **package** the band!

Photo fact!

Photographs are important for a band's image. They show what the music and the band are about.

Photographer

Make-up artist

Music videos

Music videos are a marketing tool.

Music videos really took off in the 1980s.

Music Television (MTV) started in 1981 in the US. MTV now holds award shows for music videos. Viewers vote for the winning artists.

Kelly Clarkson won Best Female Video in 2005.

Usher dances in the 'Yeah' video.

Most artists make videos to go with their records.

Good videos are part of the music. They make the message of the music stronger.

Gorillaz are the world's first **virtual band**. The video for 'Feel Good Inc.' won two MTV Video Music Awards in 2005.

Selling music

Most hit records sell best in their first week on sale.

Sales people have to guess how many CDs they will sell.

They have to send shops the right number of CDs.

They also tell shops where to get more CDs if they need them.

Today, many people download music from the Internet.

Online music stores and band websites sell music, videos and ringtones.

Download fact!

Gnarls Barkley released 'Crazy' in 2006. It was the first UK number one based on download sales alone.

Merchandising

Merchandising means selling things that have the band's name or logo on.

Many bands sell **merchandise** after gigs.

Merchandisers sell **merchandise** in shops or online. They give the band or record label a part of the **profits**.

Merchandising also advertises the band!

Ringtones

Ringtones are like **merchandise**. They make money – and they advertise the band.

People like to hear music before they buy it. Most ringtone sales are made before the record is released.

Doing it yourself

Sway is a London rapper. He won Best Hip-Hop Act at the 2005 MOBOs. He beat 50 Cent — and he wasn't signed to a label!

He recorded two albums at home.

He sold the albums on the Internet, on the streets and after gigs.

He used the money to make music videos.

The videos were shown on TV.

Sway still hasn't signed to a label.

'It isn't about greed,' he says. 'I want to see what I can create myself!'

Music fact!

In 2005, Sway wrote a song about his MySpace profile. Many other acts have used the MySpace website to advertise their music.

Quiz

1 What did Alan Wills do before he started a record label?

2 What does the name 'Reth' mean?

3 When did Arctic Monkeys make their first EP?

4 Who wrote many songs with Robbie Williams?

5 What does a booking agent do?

6 Where did Cocorosie record their first album?

7 Which DJ made Keane's first record 'Single of the Week'?

8 In which year did MTV start in the US?

9 Which record got to UK number one based on download sales alone?

10 What major award did Sway win in 2005?

Glossary of terms

classical   The sort of music performed by orchestras or choirs.

demo   Short for 'demonstration' – a demo recording shows what the band can do.

extreme metal   A fast brand of heavy-metal music.

fan base   The number of fans a band has.

interview   When someone asks questions for the band to answer.

master   The recording from which all other recordings are copied.

merchandise   Items for sale that are linked to the band or the record.

package   The total product that is sold to the buyer – the record, the band, the image, the logo and so on.

profits   The money left over when the costs have been paid.

rehearsal   Time for practising the music.

review   What someone writes or says about something they have seen, heard or read.

stylist   Person paid to dress someone else – they choose clothes for them and help them create an image.

support   Most gigs have a main band and a support act – the support act warms the crowd up for the main act.

venue   The place where a gig is held.

virtual band   A band that is not made up of real people – Gorillaz are cartoons.

More resources

Books

**The Rough Guide to iPods, iTunes and Music Online –
Edition 2**
Peter Buckley and Duncan Clark
Published by Rough Guides (ISBN: 1843535564)

Everything you need to know about downloading music.

Music (Behind Media series)
Catherine Chambers
Published by Heinemann Library (ISBN: 0431114668)

Find out about every part of the music business in this book.

Magazines

There are lots of music magazines. Here are two of
the most popular.

New Musical Express (NME) IPC Media Ltd

Mojo EMAP

Websites

http://www.bbc.co.uk/radio1/onemusic/
The Radio 1 website keeps you up to date with music.
You can also find out about the music business there.

http://www.mtv.co.uk/
Listen to music, watch videos and keep up with the gossip at the
MTV site.

DVDs and Videos

Keane – Strangers (Music Documentary) (2005)
Universal-Island (Cat. No. B000BD7NEC)
The story of Keane – from the time they formed the band at
school to the present day.

Later... with Jools Holland, Cool Britannia 2 (2005)
Warner Music Vision (Cat. No. B000AYQJ4M)
Thirty live performances from some of the UK's greatest bands –
including Kaiser Chiefs, Hard-Fi, Blur and Coldplay.

Answers

1 He was the drummer for Shack.

2 King

3 2005

4 Guy Chambers

5 Books the venues for gigs.

6 In a bathtub.

7 Steve Lamacq

8 1981

9 'Crazy' by Gnarls Barkley

10 Best Hip-Hop Act at the MOBOs.

Index